D0794296

JUN 08

GORILLAS

by Meish Goldish

Consultant: Rebecca Gullott
Collection Manager, Mammals
The Maryland Zoo in Baltimore

BEARPORT
PUBLISHING

New York, New York

Credits

Cover and Title Page, © Ken Lucas/Taxi/Getty Images; Cover (background), © Marilyn Nieves/ Istockphoto.com; 4, © Stephanie Sinclare/Chicago Tribune/NewsCom; 5, © Robert Allison/Contact Press Images; 6, © Dr. Ronald H. Cohn/Gorilla Foundation/Koko.org; 7, © Dr. Ronald H. Cohn/Gorilla Foundation/Koko.org; 8, © Dr. Ronald H. Cohn/Gorilla Foundation/Koko.org; 9T, © Dr. Ronald H. Cohn/ Gorilla Foundation/Koko.org; 9B, © Dr. Ronald H. Cohn/Gorilla Foundation/Koko.org; 10, © SHNS photo by Ron Cohn/Gorilla Foundation/Koko.org; 11, © Gorilla Foundation/Koko.org; 12, © Michael Pogany/ Columbus Zoo; 13, © Michael Pogany/Columbus Zoo; 14R, © Robert Campbell; 14L, © Yann Arthus-Bertrand/Peter Arnold, Inc.; 15, © Robert Campbell; 16, © Robert Campbell; 17, © Robert Campbell; 19, © Zigmund Leszczynski/Animals Animals - Earth Scenes; 20, © Thomas Breuer/ Wildlife Conservation; 21, © Thomas Breuer/ Wildlife Conservation; 22, © AP Images /Anjan Sundaram; 23, © William West/AFP/ Getty Images/NewsCom.com; 24, © Michael Pogany/Columbus Zoo; 25, © Michael Pogany/Columbus Zoo; 26, © Bruce Davidson/naturepl.com; 27, © Andrew Plumtree/Oxford Scientific; 28, © Steve Turner/ Photolibrary/Oxford Scientific; 29, © Sculpture by Ralph Brown/Nature In Art, UK.

Publisher: Kenn Goin
Project Editor: Adam Siegel
Creative Director: Spencer Brinker
Photo Researcher: Beaura Kathy Ringrose
Original Design: Dawn Beard Creative

Library of Congress Cataloging-in-Publication Data

Goldish, Meish.
  Gorillas / by Meish Goldish.
    p. cm. — (Smart animals!)
  Includes bibliographical references.
  ISBN-13: 978-1-59716-369-9 (library binding)
  ISBN-10: 1-59716-369-4 (library binding)
  1. Gorilla — Juvenile literature. I. Title.

  QL737.P96G565 2007
  599.884 — dc22

                    2006026657

For more information, write to Bearport Publishing Company, Inc., 101 Fifth Avenue, Suite 6R, New York, New York 10003. Printed in the United States of America.

10 9 8 7 6 5 4 3 2 1

Contents

Gorilla to the Rescue

Visitors at the Brookfield Zoo in Illinois watched with fear. A three-year-old boy lay **unconscious** at the bottom of the gorilla **exhibit**. He had fallen 18 feet (5 m) while trying to climb over the railing. Soon a gorilla named Binti Jua (BIN-tee JOO-ah) walked toward the boy. Would she attack him?

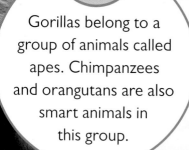

Gorillas belong to a group of animals called apes. Chimpanzees and orangutans are also smart animals in this group.

▲ Binti Jua

The gorilla surprised everyone. She gently scooped up the boy and carried him to a door where help waited.

Binti Jua became famous for rescuing a human. She had acted like a loving mother. Her actions changed many people's ideas about gorillas. They had thought of gorillas as **savage** beasts. Now they saw them as gentle, **intelligent** creatures.

▲ **Binti Jua's rescue of a three-year-old boy was captured on video.**

Language Learner

Binti Jua is just one of many gorillas that have shown people how smart they are. In 1971, Koko was born at the San Francisco Zoo. When she was a year old, Koko became the first gorilla to learn **American Sign Language**.

▲ **Koko learns new words by having her hands moved into the positions that stand for the words.**

The young gorilla was taught that different hand movements stand for different words. At first, Koko was only able to **sign** one word at a time, such as "drink," "food," or "more." By age three, she was smart enough to sign sentences made up of three to six words. When she was thirsty, Koko signed, "Pour that hurry drink hurry."

By age five, Koko could sign more than 200 words. A child who is two and a half years old knows about the same number of words.

▲ **One of the first words Koko learned to sign was "food."**

Koko's Kitten

Over the years, Koko learned to sign more than 1,000 words. She used her hands to express her feelings and needs.

In 1984, Koko received a pet kitten, which she named All Ball. Koko's teacher asked her to tell a story about her kitten. Koko signed, "Koko love Ball. Soft good cat cat." When Koko held the kitten, she saw its claws. "Cat do scratch," the gorilla signed.

▲ **Koko and All Ball**

Koko can have a conversation with a person by signing her thoughts. Yet Koko understands more than just sign language. She also understands about 2,000 words of spoken English.

◀ **Koko signing "toothbrush"**

The easiest words for Koko to learn were the names of things, such as "hat," "key," and "ball." Next she learned action words, such as "chase" and "bite."

▲ **Koko signing "tree"**

Picture This

Koko isn't the only gorilla that has learned to **communicate** with humans. Koko's friend, Michael, also learned to use sign language. Yet Michael had another talent as well. He painted amazing pictures.

Chimpanzees, elephants, and sea lions are other smart animals that have been taught to paint.

▲ **Michael working on a painting**

Sometimes Michael seemed to follow a plan when he painted. Once, he painted a picture of a toy dinosaur that had spikes. First he painted the dinosaur's body. Then he flipped the painting over and pressed it onto the floor with the paint side down. Next, he slowly picked up the painting so that a bumpy **texture** was created on the dinosaur's body. Now his dinosaur had spikes!

Michael also painted a picture of his pet dog, Apple. The painting looks similar to the dog's face.

▲ **Michael's painting of his pet dog**

Gorilla Feelings

Painting involves a gorilla's **physical** skill and intelligence. Yet gorillas also have **emotional** intelligence, just like humans. They are able to feel love, joy, fear, and jealousy.

Bridgette and Bongo lived with their son, Fossey, at the Columbus Zoo in Ohio. When Bridgette died, Bongo **grieved** deeply. He sat in his cage, calling to her again and again.

▲ **Bridgette and Fossey**

After Bridgette's death, zookeepers feared that Bongo would ignore his son. Instead, Bongo showed great care. He was able to look after Fossey by himself. Bongo even made his son's bed of hay each night, just as Bridgette used to do.

When a gorilla is sad or hurt, it will cry. However, it cries by making sounds, not tears.

▲ **After Bridgette's death, Bongo was a responsible parent to his 14-month-old son, Fossey.**

Watching in the Wild

Fossey, the baby gorilla that lived at the Columbus Zoo, was named for Dian Fossey. She was an American **zoologist** who spent almost 18 years studying gorillas in the African mountains. By observing the animals in their natural **habitat**, she found out just how smart wild gorillas really are.

▲ Dian Fossey spent thousands of hours in Africa observing gorillas.

▲ In order to be accepted by gorillas, Dian Fossey chewed on the same vegetables as they did, made the same noises, beat her chest, and scratched her head.

Dian Fossey wasn't sure what the gorillas might do when they saw her watching them. She gained their trust by copying their sounds, movements, and actions.

Dian Fossey named each gorilla she studied. She made history in 1970 when she touched hands with Peanuts. It was the first time a human was ever known to have touched a wild mountain gorilla!

◀ **Dian Fossey extends a hand toward Peanuts.**

Gorillas identify one another by their faces and body shapes. Scientists use a gorilla's nose print to identify an animal. Like human fingerprints, no two nose prints are the same.

Sounds and Meanings

Dian Fossey found that gorillas use different sounds to communicate with one another. A male gorilla will cry *Wraagh* to announce his arrival in an area. He means "Don't worry, it's only me." The sound *Naoom, naoom* means "Food is here. Come and get it." An adult male will grunt like a pig to settle a disagreement. When curious, a gorilla may make a hooting sound.

▲ **Dian Fossey discovered that gorillas make special sounds to express joy. This gorilla chuckles as Fossey tickles him.**

A gorilla's **belch** means "I'm happy." Gorillas nearby will then belch back. The animals use these sounds to keep track of one another. Beware of a short belch, however. That is the sound adult gorillas use to tell their young to behave!

Gorillas use at least 25 different sounds to communicate with one another.

▲ Fossey used a tape recorder to capture all the different sounds gorillas make to communicate.

Smart Games

Dian Fossey studied mountain gorillas. Two other kinds of gorillas are eastern lowland gorillas and western lowland gorillas. All three kinds live in Africa.

Gorillas in the Wild

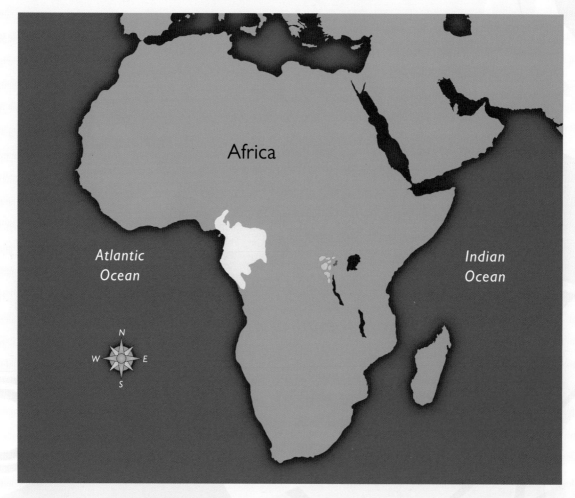

▲ **Gorillas in the wild are found in different parts of Central Africa. This map shows where they live.**

☐ Where western lowland gorillas live
☐ Where eastern lowland gorillas live
■ Where mountain gorillas live

Gorillas live in a group, usually with 5 to 30 members. An adult male is called a silverback because of the silvery gray hair on his back. He leads and protects his **troop**. The silverback decides where the troop will eat, travel, and play.

Playing is an important activity for young gorillas. Their games often involve copying adult actions, such as breaking branches and building nests. Such games are a smart and fun way for gorillas to learn the skills they will need as adults.

▲ **Young gorillas playing**

Young gorillas enjoy playing King of the Hill. As players try to knock one another off a mound, they learn how to defend themselves.

Using Tools

Using **tools** is another sign of a smart animal. Until recently, scientists didn't think that gorillas in the wild used tools. In 2004, however, a female gorilla in Africa named Leah showed them they were wrong.

▲ **Leah used a long tree branch to test the depth of water.**

Like gorillas, other smart animals such as crows, dolphins, elephants, and chimpanzees have shown that they can use tools in the wild.

Leah wanted to cross a pool of water. Yet she wasn't sure if the water was too deep. So she used a tool to find out. Leah picked up a thin tree branch. She then placed it in the water to test the water's depth. Leah kept checking the water with the stick as she walked.

▲ Efi is another gorilla that used a tool. She leaned on a branch to keep her balance as she searched for food.

Clever Cracking

Gorillas don't use just plants and branches as tools. At least one of these clever creatures also found a way to use rocks. A female gorilla named Itebero (*eet-uh-BAIR-oh*) was seen smashing palm nuts with rocks to get the oil inside. Scientists were amazed. They thought only humans and chimpanzees could use rocks as tools.

▲ **Itebero used rocks to smash open hard nuts.**

Itebero was living in an animal **sanctuary** in Africa. Gorillas learn a lot by copying the actions of others. So some scientists thought Itebero might have learned her nut-cracking skills from watching humans. However, she had never seen anyone cracking nuts. Itebero figured out how to use rocks as tools all by herself!

Like humans, gorillas have four fingers and a thumb on each hand. This kind of hand lets humans and gorillas pick up and hold objects that they can use as tools.

Learning by Watching

No one taught Itebero how to crack nuts. Baron Macombo, however, showed how a clever gorilla can learn by watching others. He and two other gorillas were being moved to a different area at a zoo. Zookeepers used food to **lure** the first two gorillas into wooden crates with a trap door. Baron Macombo watched how his friends were tricked.

▲ **Christopher and Millie Christina were easily led into crates after seeing food in them.**

Now it was Baron Macombo's turn to go inside a crate. He reached for the food, just as the others had done. However, he was smart enough to hold the trap door open with his leg at the same time. He grabbed the food and stepped outside without being captured!

▲ **Baron Macombo was too clever to get caught inside his crate.**

Baron Macombo watched other gorillas to figure out how to get food out of a crate without getting caught inside. Learning how to solve a problem is a sign of a smart animal.

Staying Alive

Gorillas like Baron Macombo live in the safety of a zoo. However, gorillas in the African wild face serious dangers. They are clever animals, yet hunters can still harm them. **Poachers** kill many gorillas for food or sell their body parts as **souvenirs**. Gorillas are now in danger of becoming **extinct**.

▲ **Park rangers in Africa carry away the body of a gorilla that was killed by poachers.**

In Africa, laws have been passed to protect gorillas. It is now **illegal** to hunt them. Yet poachers continue to kill them. Mountain gorillas are now listed as an **endangered species**.

Today, many people are working to ensure the safety of gorillas. With their help, these intelligent animals will continue to survive.

▲ **A gorilla that has been hurt is getting medical help.**

Humans are a big threat to gorilla survival. They cut down trees and use the apes' land for farming so that the gorillas have fewer places to live.

Just the Facts

Mountain Gorilla

Weight	males: 297–605 pounds (135–274 kg) females: 154–308 pounds (70–140 kg)
Height	males: up to about 6 feet (1.8 m) when standing females: up to about 5 feet (1.5 m) when standing
Food	leaves, tree bark, roots, shoots, flowers, vines, and fruits
Life Span	30–50 years
Habitat	African rain forests high in the Virunga Mountains
Population	about 740 in the wild; 0 in captivity

More Smart Gorillas

At the Columbus Zoo in Ohio, a gorilla named Colo found a child's set of plastic keys. Zookeepers worried that the gorilla might choke on them. They offered to trade a spoonful of ice cream for the keys. Wanting more ice cream than that, Colo broke the key chain and offered just one key in return. It took many spoonfuls of ice cream to get all the keys back!

In Europe, a five-year-old boy fell into the gorilla exhibit at the Jersey Zoo. Several curious gorillas began to move closer to the unconscious boy. One gorilla named Jambo placed himself between the boy and the other gorillas, as if to say "Don't touch." He gently stroked the boy, who soon awoke and was taken to a hospital. A statue of Jambo was placed at the zoo in his honor.

▲ **A statue of Jambo**

29

Glossary

American Sign Language (uh-MER-uh-kuhn SINE LANG-gwij) a language that is used instead of spoken words; it is made up of hand and body movements, as well as facial expressions, and is often used by people who can't hear

belch (BELCH) a noise made by letting out air from the stomach through the mouth

communicate (kuh-MYOO-nuh-kate) to share information, wants, needs, and feelings

emotional (i-MOH-shuh-nuhl) having to do with one's feelings

endangered species (en-DAYN-jurd SPEE-sheez) a kind of animal that is in danger of dying out

exhibit (eg-ZIB-it) something that is shown to the public

extinct (ek-STINGKT) when a kind of animal has died out; when there are no more alive on Earth

grieved (GREEVD) felt very sad

habitat (HAB-uh-*tat*) a place in nature where an animal is usually found

illegal (i-LEE-guhl) against the law

intelligent (in-TEL-uh-juhnt) smart

lure (LOOR) to attract or lead someone into a trap

physical (FIZ-uh-kuhl) having to do with the body

poachers (POHCH-urz) people who hunt illegally

sanctuary (SANGK-choo-er-ee) an area in nature where animals are protected from hunters

savage (SAV-ij) dangerous or violent

sign (SINE) to make hand movements that stand for words

souvenirs (*soo*-vuh-NIHRZ) objects that remind people of something

texture (TEKS-chur) the way something looks and feels

tools (TOOLZ) equipment that is used to do a job

troop (TROOP) a group of gorillas that live together

unconscious (uhn-KON-shuhss) not awake; unable to think, hear, feel, or see

zoologist (zoh-OL-uh-jist) someone who studies animal life

Bibliography

Matthews, Tom L. *Light Shining Through the Mist: A Photobiography of Dian Fossey.* Washington, D.C.: National Geographic Society (1998).

Miller-Schroeder, Patricia. *Gorillas.* Austin, TX: Raintree Steck-Vaughn (1997).

Redmond, Ian. *Gorilla, Monkey & Ape.* New York: Dorling Kindersley (2000).

Taylor, Marianne. *Mountain Gorilla.* Chicago: Heinemann Library (2004).

Read More

Lewin, Ted, and Betsy Lewin. *Gorilla Walk.* New York: Lothrop, Lee & Shepard (1999).

Mara, Wil. *Dian Fossey: Among the Gorillas.* New York: Franklin Watts (2004).

Patterson, Dr. Francine. *Koko-Love!: Conversations with a Signing Gorilla.* New York: Dutton Children's Books (1999).

Simon, Seymour. *Gorillas.* New York: HarperTrophy (2000).

Learn More Online

To learn more about gorillas, visit
www.bearportpublishing.com/SmartAnimals

Index

About the Author

Meish Goldish has written
more than 100 books for children.